# Mastering Apple Vision Pro
# -The Ultimate User's Guide

# Step-by-Step Instructions to
# Get Started

## By

## Aurora Voss

# Contents

# Introduction

This guide is designed to help you master the Apple Vision Pro, from unboxing to advanced features. It provides clear, step-by-step instructions to ensure you get the most out of your device. This guide is for all users, whether you're a beginner just getting started or an advanced user looking to deepen your knowledge and skills with the Apple Vision Pro. Each chapter in this book builds on the previous one, starting with basic setup and progressing to more advanced topics. You can follow it sequentially for a comprehensive understanding or jump to specific sections as needed. Apple Vision Pro is a cutting-edge wearable device that integrates advanced visual and audio technology to enhance user interaction. It features a high-resolution display, spatial audio, and intuitive controls designed to provide an immersive experience.

## Key Features and Benefits

- **High-Resolution Display:** Provides crystal-clear visuals for all your activities.

- **Spatial Audio:** Delivers immersive sound quality that adapts to your environment.

- **Intuitive Controls:** Easy-to-use touch and voice controls for seamless interaction.

- **Augmented Reality (AR) Capabilities:** Enhances your real-world experience with interactive digital elements.

- **Connectivity Options:** Includes Wi-Fi, Bluetooth, and seamless integration with other Apple devices.

- **Health and Fitness Monitoring:** Tracks your health metrics and offers guided workouts to help you stay fit.
- **Privacy and Security:** Advanced security features like Face ID and customizable privacy settings to protect your data.

This guide will walk you through all these features and more, ensuring you can leverage the full potential of your Apple Vision Pro.

# Chapter 1: Getting Started with Apple Vision Pro

**Unboxing and Setup**

When you unbox your Apple Vision Pro, you'll find several components neatly arranged inside. The primary item is the Apple Vision Pro device itself, which features a high-resolution display and integrated spatial audio system designed to offer an immersive user experience. Alongside the device, you'll discover a USB-C charging cable and a power adapter to keep your device powered. Additionally, the package includes adjustable headbands and various fitting accessories to ensure the device fits comfortably on different head shapes and sizes. A quick start guide is provided to help you get up and running quickly, along with warranty and safety information that outlines the terms of service and important safety precautions.

The initial setup and configuration process begins with powering on the device by pressing and holding the power button until the Apple logo appears.

You'll then be prompted to select your preferred language and region from the available options. Connecting to Wi-Fi is the next step; choose your Wi-Fi network from the list and enter the password to establish a connection. Signing in with your Apple ID is crucial for accessing Apple services; if you don't have an Apple ID, you can create one during this step. Setting up Face ID follows, where you'll need to follow on-screen instructions to ensure your device is secure and easily accessible. After setting up Face ID, you can customize various settings such as display brightness, sound levels, and notification preferences to suit your needs. It's also recommended to download essential apps from the App Store to enhance your experience, such as communication, productivity, and entertainment apps. Finally, check for any available software updates and install them to ensure your device has the latest features and security improvements. Familiarize yourself with the home screen layout, including app icons, widgets, and the control center, to start using your Apple Vision Pro efficiently. By following these steps, you will have your Apple Vision Pro set up and ready for use, ensuring an optimal starting experience with your new device.

**Navigating the Interface**

Navigating the interface of the Apple Vision Pro starts with understanding the home screen, which is your primary hub for accessing apps and features. The home screen displays app icons in a grid layout, allowing you to quickly find and launch your favorite applications. At the bottom of the screen, you will find the dock, a customizable space where you can place your most frequently used apps for easy access. The status bar at the top of the screen shows essential information such as battery life, Wi-Fi connectivity, and the time.

Customizing your interface is straightforward and enhances your user experience by allowing you to tailor the device to your preferences. You can rearrange app icons on the home screen by pressing and holding an icon until it starts to jiggle, then dragging it to your desired location. Creating folders is also possible by dragging one app icon over another, making it easier to organize your apps into categories. Additionally, you can change the wallpaper by navigating to the settings menu, selecting "Wallpaper," and choosing from the available options or using your own photos. Widgets can be added to the home screen by swiping to the right and tapping the "+" icon, providing quick access to information like weather, calendar events, and news updates. Notification settings can be customized to manage how and when you receive alerts, ensuring you only get notifications that are important to you. By taking advantage of these customization options, you can make the Apple Vision Pro interface work best for your needs, providing a more efficient and personalized experience.

## Basic Operations

Using the touch controls on the Apple Vision Pro is intuitive and straightforward. The device is equipped with a high-precision touch interface that allows you to interact with it using various gestures. To navigate through the device, you can swipe left or right to switch between home screens, swipe up to access the app switcher, and swipe down from the top-right corner to open the control center where you can adjust settings like brightness, volume, and connectivity options. Tapping an app icon will open the application, while pressing and holding an icon will enable you to rearrange or delete apps. Pinch gestures can be used to zoom in and out on photos or webpages, and a double-tap can quickly zoom into specific areas.

Voice commands and gestures add another layer of convenience and accessibility to the Apple Vision Pro. The device supports Siri, Apple's virtual assistant, which you can activate by saying "Hey Siri" or by pressing and holding the side button. With Siri, you can perform a wide range of tasks using just your voice, such as setting reminders, sending messages, making phone calls, and controlling smart home devices. Gestures are also integrated into the user experience, allowing for hands-free operation. For instance, you can use head movements to scroll through content or nod to select items, enhancing usability for various situations. These basic operations make interacting with the Apple Vision Pro efficient and user-friendly, ensuring you can access its powerful features with ease.

# Chapter 2: Core Features and Functionalities

## Display and Visuals

The Apple Vision Pro boasts a high-resolution Retina display designed to deliver sharp, vibrant visuals. Adjusting display settings is essential to optimizing your viewing experience. You can adjust the brightness level by swiping down from the top-right corner to access the Control Center and using the brightness slider. Additionally, the display settings menu offers options to enable True Tone, which automatically adjusts the screen's color balance based on ambient lighting, reducing eye strain and providing more natural visuals. You can also toggle Night Shift to reduce blue light exposure during evening hours, promoting better sleep. In the same settings menu, you can adjust text size and display zoom to make content easier to read and navigate.

Using the Retina display takes full advantage of its high pixel density and color accuracy. This display technology ensures that images and text appear crisp and clear, enhancing your overall user experience. Whether you are watching videos, browsing the web, or reading documents, the Retina display provides exceptional detail and color fidelity. The display is also designed to minimize reflections and glare, making it easier to use in various lighting conditions. By customizing and utilizing these display features, you can enjoy a visually stunning and comfortable experience with your Apple Vision Pro.

**Audio and Sound**

Setting up spatial audio on the Apple Vision Pro is essential for an immersive audio experience. Spatial audio uses dynamic head tracking to create a surround sound effect, making it feel as if the sound is coming from all around you. To set up spatial audio, go to the settings menu, select "Sound," and then "Spatial Audio." Ensure that it is toggled on. You can also test the spatial audio feature with supported content by playing a compatible video or audio track. This feature enhances your experience when watching movies, playing games, or listening to music by providing a more realistic and engaging sound environment.

Customizing sound preferences allows you to tailor the audio output to your liking. In the sound settings menu, you can adjust the volume balance between the left and right channels to suit your hearing preferences. The equalizer settings let you modify the sound profile by enhancing bass, treble, or mid-range frequencies, ensuring that the audio output matches your personal taste. Additionally, you can enable features like "Reduce Loud Sounds" to automatically lower the volume of loud noises, protecting your hearing and providing a more consistent listening experience. These customization options ensure that the audio experience on your Apple Vision Pro is optimized for comfort and enjoyment, whether you are using it for entertainment, communication, or productivity.

**Connectivity and Networking**

Connecting to Wi-Fi and Bluetooth on the Apple Vision Pro is straightforward and ensures you stay connected to the internet and your other devices. To connect to Wi-Fi, open the settings menu, select "Wi-Fi," and choose your network from the list of available options. Enter the password if required, and your device will connect to the network. For Bluetooth, go to the settings menu, select "Bluetooth," and toggle it on. Your device will automatically scan for nearby Bluetooth devices. Select the device you want to connect to from the list, and follow any additional prompts to pair them.

Using AirDrop and Continuity features enhances your ability to share and sync content seamlessly across your Apple devices. AirDrop allows you to quickly share files, photos, and other content with nearby Apple devices. To use AirDrop, ensure both Wi-Fi and Bluetooth are enabled on your device. Then, open the file you want to share, tap the share icon, and select the AirDrop option. Choose the recipient's device from the list, and they will receive a notification to accept the transfer. Continuity features enable seamless integration between your Apple Vision Pro and other Apple devices, such as Macs, iPads, and iPhones. This includes the ability to start an email or document on one device and finish it on another, make and receive phone calls, and send SMS messages from your Apple Vision Pro. To use Continuity, ensure all your devices are signed in with the same Apple

ID and have Wi-Fi and Bluetooth enabled. These connectivity features enhance the functionality of your Apple Vision Pro, making it easy to stay connected and productive across your Apple ecosystem.

# Chapter 3: Productivity and Applications

**Built-In Apps Overview**

The Apple Vision Pro comes equipped with several built-in apps designed to enhance productivity and keep you organized.

Notes and Reminders are two essential apps for managing your tasks and ideas. The Notes app allows you to create, organize, and edit notes with text, images, and sketches. You can also use folders and tags to keep your notes sorted. The Reminders app helps you manage tasks and to-dos, offering features like due dates, priority levels, and location-based reminders. These apps sync across all your Apple devices via iCloud, ensuring you have access to your notes and reminders wherever you are.

Calendar and Mail are key for managing your schedule and communications. The Calendar app lets you create and manage events, set alerts, and invite others to meetings. You can view your schedule by day, week, or month, and sync your calendars from various accounts such as iCloud, Google, and Exchange. The Mail app integrates with multiple email services, providing a unified inbox for all your email accounts. It supports features like threaded conversations, VIP contacts, and customizable notifications. With Calendar and Mail, you can stay on top of your appointments and correspondence, ensuring you are always organized and informed. These built-in apps are designed to streamline your workflow and boost your productivity with the Apple Vision Pro.

## Using Third-Party Apps

Using third-party apps on the Apple Vision Pro expands the functionality of your device beyond the built-in apps. Installing new apps is simple and can be done through the App Store. Open the App Store app, browse or search for the app you need, and tap the "Get" or price button to download and install it. Once installed, the app icon will appear on your home screen, ready for use.

Managing app permissions is crucial for maintaining your privacy and security. When you first open a newly installed app, it may request access to various features or data, such as your location, contacts, or microphone. Carefully review these requests and grant permissions only if necessary for the app's functionality. You can manage and adjust these permissions at any time by going to the settings menu, selecting "Privacy," and then choosing the relevant category (e.g., Location Services, Contacts, Microphone). Here, you can see a list of apps that have requested access and toggle permissions on or off as needed. By managing app permissions, you ensure that your personal information is protected while still enjoying the full capabilities of third-party apps on your Apple Vision Pro.

**Multitasking and Workflow**

Multitasking and workflow optimization on the Apple Vision Pro are facilitated through features like Split View, Slide Over, the Dock, and the App Switcher.

Split View and Slide Over allow you to use multiple apps simultaneously. In Split View, you can display two apps side by side, making it easy to work on tasks like taking notes while reading an article. To activate Split View, open an app, swipe up from the bottom of the screen to reveal the Dock, then drag a second app from the Dock to the left or right edge of the screen. Adjust the divider between the apps to resize them as needed. Slide Over lets you open a third app in a floating window over your main app. To use Slide Over, drag an app from the Dock to the center of the screen and release. You can move the Slide Over window to either side of the screen by dragging it, and dismiss it by swiping it off the screen.

Using the Dock and App Switcher enhances your ability to quickly access and manage your apps. The Dock, located at the bottom of the home screen, holds your most frequently used apps for quick access. You can add or remove apps from the Dock by dragging them in or out. The App Switcher allows you to view and switch between recently used apps. To access the App Switcher, swipe up from the bottom of the screen and pause in the middle, or double-click the home button. This view shows all open apps in a grid format, enabling you to tap on any app to switch to it or swipe up to close an app.

By utilizing Split View, Slide Over, the Dock, and the App Switcher, you can efficiently manage multiple tasks and streamline your workflow on the Apple Vision Pro.

# Chapter 4: Enhanced Reality and Entertainment

**Augmented Reality Experiences**

Augmented Reality (AR) on the Apple Vision Pro offers immersive experiences that blend digital content with the real world. Setting up AR applications involves a few simple steps. First, download AR apps from the App Store that are compatible with your device. Once installed, open the app and grant necessary permissions, such as camera access, to enable AR functionalities. The app will guide you through the initial setup, which often includes calibrating your environment by moving your device around to scan the area.

Best practices for AR usage ensure a safe and enjoyable experience. Always use AR applications in well-lit, open spaces free of obstacles to avoid accidents. Be mindful of your surroundings and maintain awareness of real-world hazards. It's also important to take regular breaks to avoid eye strain, especially during prolonged use. Additionally, keep your device's software updated to benefit from the latest AR enhancements and security improvements. By following these guidelines, you can maximize the potential of AR applications on your Apple Vision Pro, enjoying interactive and engaging augmented reality experiences safely and effectively.

## Media Consumption

Media consumption on the Apple Vision Pro is seamless and immersive, allowing you to enjoy streaming movies and music, as well as viewing your personal photos and videos.

Streaming Movies and Music involves using apps like Apple TV, Netflix, and Apple Music. To stream movies, open the Apple TV app or any other streaming service you subscribe to, browse or search for the content you want to watch, and tap play. For music, open Apple Music or your preferred streaming app, find your favorite songs or playlists, and start streaming. You can adjust playback settings, such as volume and playback speed, directly within these apps for a personalized experience. The high-resolution display and spatial audio features of the Apple Vision Pro enhance the quality of your media consumption, providing clear visuals and immersive sound.

Using the Photos and Videos Apps allows you to organize and enjoy your personal media. The Photos app automatically sorts your photos and videos into albums based on date, location, and other criteria. You can browse through your media, create custom albums, and edit photos and videos using built-in tools. To view a photo or video, simply tap on it to open it in full screen. The app also supports sharing options, enabling you to easily share your favorite moments with friends and family via social media or messaging apps. Additionally, the Photos app offers features like Memories and Live Photos, which bring your images to life by creating curated collections and short animations.

By utilizing these features, you can fully enjoy the diverse media capabilities of your Apple Vision Pro, whether you are streaming the latest movies and music or reliving personal moments through your photos and videos.

**Gaming and Interactive Content**

Downloading Games on the Apple Vision Pro is a straightforward process that opens up a world of entertainment. To download games, open the App Store app and browse or search for the games you are interested in. Once you find a game, tap the "Get" or price button to download and install it. The game icon will appear on your home screen once the installation is complete, ready for you to launch and play. Many games on the App

Store are optimized for the Vision Pro's high-resolution display and spatial audio, providing an immersive gaming experience.

Enhancing Gameplay with Vision Pro involves taking advantage of the device's advanced features. The high-resolution Retina display ensures crisp and vibrant visuals, making games more engaging. Spatial audio enhances the auditory experience by providing dynamic, 3D sound, making it feel like you are part of the game's environment. The Vision Pro's powerful processor ensures smooth gameplay, even for graphically intensive games. Additionally, the device supports various gaming accessories like Bluetooth controllers, which can be connected through the Bluetooth settings for more precise control and an enhanced gaming experience. Utilizing these features maximizes your gaming enjoyment, providing a rich and immersive interactive content experience on the Apple Vision Pro.

# Chapter 5:
# Communication and
# Collaboration

## Video and Voice Calls

Setting up FaceTime on the Apple Vision Pro allows you to make high-quality video and voice calls with other Apple device users. To set up FaceTime, open the FaceTime app and sign in with your Apple ID. You can then add contacts by entering their phone numbers or email addresses. To make a call, simply select a contact and choose either a video or audio call. FaceTime also supports group calls, allowing you to connect with multiple people simultaneously. Ensure you have a stable internet connection for the best call quality.

Using third-party communication apps expands your calling options to include non-Apple users. Popular apps like Zoom, Skype, and WhatsApp can be downloaded from the App Store. Once installed, open the app and follow the setup instructions, which typically involve creating an account or signing in with existing credentials. These apps also allow you to add contacts, make voice and video calls, and participate in group conversations. Each app has its unique features, such as virtual backgrounds in Zoom or end-to-end encryption in WhatsApp, enhancing your communication experience. By using FaceTime and third-party apps, you can stay connected with friends, family, and colleagues, ensuring seamless communication and collaboration on your Apple Vision Pro.

**Sharing and Collaboration Tools**

Using SharePlay on the Apple Vision Pro allows you to share experiences in real-time with others during FaceTime calls. With SharePlay, you can watch movies, listen to music, or view apps together with friends and family. To use SharePlay, start a FaceTime call and then open a compatible app, such as Apple TV or Apple Music. Tap the SharePlay button to begin sharing the content with everyone on the call. Participants can control playback, and you can enjoy synchronized media, making it feel like you are together even when apart.

Collaborating on documents and projects is made easy with built-in and third-party apps. Apple's iWork suite, which includes Pages, Numbers, and Keynote, allows real-time collaboration on documents, spreadsheets, and presentations. To collaborate, open the document in one of these apps, tap the share button, and invite others to join by entering their email addresses. You can set permissions for viewing or editing and see changes in real-time as collaborators make updates. Third-party apps like Google Docs, Microsoft Office, and Dropbox Paper also support collaborative work. These apps can be downloaded from the App Store and offer similar real-time editing and sharing features. By leveraging SharePlay and collaboration tools, you can efficiently work together with others, enhancing productivity and teamwork on your Apple Vision Pro.

**Social Media Integration**

Connecting to social media accounts on the Apple Vision Pro allows you to stay updated and interact with your networks. To connect your accounts, download your preferred social media apps from the App Store, such as Facebook, Twitter, Instagram, or LinkedIn. Once installed, open the app and sign in with your credentials. These apps may request permissions to access your contacts, photos, and notifications, which you can grant to enhance your experience.

Using social media apps on the Apple Vision Pro is straightforward and takes full advantage of the device's features. The high-resolution display makes browsing feeds, viewing photos, and watching videos enjoyable. You can post updates, share photos, comment on posts, and send messages directly through these apps. Notifications will keep you informed about likes, comments, and messages, ensuring you stay connected with your social network. Additionally, the Vision Pro's powerful processor ensures smooth performance, even with media-rich content. By connecting to and using social media apps, you can efficiently manage your online presence and engage with your community on the Apple Vision Pro.

# Chapter 6: Health and Fitness

**Health Monitoring Features**

Setting up health metrics on the Apple Vision Pro involves configuring the Health app to track various health parameters. Open the Health app and enter your personal information such as age, weight, and height. You can then select the health metrics you want to monitor, such as heart rate, activity levels, and sleep patterns. The device will use its built-in sensors to collect data and provide insights into your overall health. Ensure that you grant necessary permissions for the app to access and record health data.

Using the Fitness app on the Apple Vision Pro enhances your fitness routine by providing personalized workout recommendations and tracking your progress. Open the Fitness app, sign in with your Apple ID, and set your fitness goals, such as the number of calories you want to burn, the amount of exercise, and how often you stand each day. The app offers various workout options, including guided workouts, and tracks your activity through metrics like steps taken, distance traveled, and calories burned. You can view detailed summaries of your workouts and overall activity levels, helping you stay motivated and achieve your fitness goals. By setting up health metrics and using the Fitness app, you can effectively monitor and improve your health and fitness with the Apple Vision Pro.

**Guided Workouts and Exercises**

Accessing workout programs on the Apple Vision Pro is straightforward and offers a variety of exercise options to suit your fitness needs. Open the Fitness app, navigate to the "Workouts" section, and browse the available programs. You can choose from a range of guided workouts, including yoga, strength training, cardio, and more. Each workout program provides detailed instructions and video demonstrations to ensure proper form and technique. Select a workout, and follow along with the guidance provided.

Tracking progress and achievements is an integral part of maintaining motivation and measuring your fitness improvements. The Fitness app automatically records your workout data, such as duration, calories burned, and heart rate. You can view this data in real-time during your workout and access detailed summaries afterward. The app also tracks your daily activity, displaying rings for Move, Exercise, and Stand goals, which you aim to close each day. Additionally, the Fitness app offers achievements and awards for reaching milestones and completing challenges, providing extra motivation to stay active. By accessing guided workout programs and consistently tracking your progress and achievements, you can effectively manage and enhance your fitness journey with the Apple Vision Pro.

# Chapter 7: Security and Privacy

**Setting Up Security Features**

Setting up security features on the Apple Vision Pro is crucial for protecting your personal information and ensuring privacy. Start by setting up Face ID, which uses facial recognition to unlock your device securely. To set up Face ID, go to the settings menu, select "Face ID & Passcode," and follow the on-screen instructions to scan your face. This process ensures that only you can access your device. Additionally, set up a strong password as a backup security measure by navigating to "Settings," then "Face ID & Passcode," and selecting "Change Passcode."

Configuring privacy settings is essential to control what information your apps can access and share. In the settings menu, select "Privacy" to view and adjust permissions for various data categories such as location services, contacts, and photos. Review each category and toggle off any permissions that are unnecessary or that you are uncomfortable sharing. You can also manage which apps have access to sensitive data by selecting specific apps and adjusting their permissions. By setting up Face ID, password protection, and carefully configuring privacy settings, you can ensure that your Apple Vision Pro remains secure and your personal information is protected.

**Managing Permissions and Data**

Managing permissions and data on the Apple Vision Pro ensures your personal information remains secure and your privacy is maintained.

App Permissions allow you to control what information apps can access. To manage app permissions, go to the settings menu and select "Privacy." Here, you will see a list of data categories such as location services, contacts, photos, microphone, and more. Tap on each category to view which apps have requested access and toggle permissions on or off as needed. This allows you to grant or deny access to your personal information based on your preferences and the necessity of the app's functionality.

Data and Privacy Reports provide transparency about how your data is being used. In the settings menu, select "Privacy" and then "Data & Privacy." This section provides an overview of your data usage and privacy settings. You can review reports on which apps have accessed your data, what data has been shared, and how often. This helps you monitor and manage the data collected by your apps, ensuring that your privacy preferences are respected. Regularly reviewing these reports allows you to stay informed about your data privacy and make necessary adjustments to your settings.

By carefully managing app permissions and regularly reviewing data and privacy reports, you can maintain control over your personal information and ensure your Apple Vision Pro is used securely and responsibly.

## Troubleshooting Security Issues

Troubleshooting security issues on the Apple Vision Pro involves addressing common security problems and following best practices for data protection. Common Security Problems include issues such as unauthorized access, malware, and phishing attacks. If you suspect unauthorized access, immediately change your device passcode and Apple ID password. Ensure Face ID is properly set up and functioning. For malware concerns, regularly update your device to the latest software version, as updates often include security patches. If you encounter suspicious emails or messages, do not click on links or download attachments, and report the phishing attempts to Apple.

Best Practices for Data Protection help maintain the security of your personal information. Always use a strong, unique password for your Apple ID and enable two-factor authentication for an additional layer of security. Regularly back up your data to iCloud to prevent data loss. Be cautious about granting app permissions and only download apps from the App Store to avoid installing malicious software. Keep your device's software up to date to benefit from the latest security enhancements. Additionally, review your privacy settings periodically to ensure they align with your preferences.

By addressing common security problems promptly and adhering to best practices for data protection, you can effectively safeguard your Apple Vision Pro and personal information from security threats.

# Chapter 8: Advanced Settings and Customization

**System Preferences**

Configuring general settings on the Apple Vision Pro allows you to personalize your device according to your preferences. To access general settings, go to the settings menu and select "General." Here, you can adjust various settings such as language and region, date and time, and keyboard preferences. You can also manage storage, view software updates, and reset settings if needed. Configuring these settings ensures your device operates smoothly and aligns with your personal needs.

Accessibility options are designed to make the Apple Vision Pro usable for everyone, including those with disabilities. To configure accessibility options, go to the settings menu and select "Accessibility." This section offers a range of features such as VoiceOver, which provides spoken descriptions of on-screen elements; Zoom, which enlarges portions of the screen; and Magnifier, which turns your device into a digital magnifying glass. You can also adjust display settings to reduce motion, increase contrast, or enable color filters. For those with hearing impairments, options like Live Listen and mono audio are available. Customizing these settings ensures that the device is accessible and user-friendly for all users. Configuring general settings and utilizing accessibility options, you can fully customize the Apple Vision Pro to meet your specific needs and preferences, enhancing your overall user experience.

**Customizing the User Experience**

Customizing the user experience on the Apple Vision Pro involves changing themes and wallpapers and customizing notifications to suit your preferences. Changing Themes and Wallpapers allows you to personalize the look and feel of your device. To change the wallpaper, go to the settings menu, select "Wallpaper," and then choose either "Choose a New Wallpaper" or select from your photos. You can set different wallpapers for the home screen and lock screen. Additionally, the Apple Vision Pro supports dark and light themes. To switch between these themes, go to the settings menu, select "Display & Brightness," and choose either "Light" or "Dark" mode. You can also set it to automatically switch based on the time of day.

Customizing Notifications ensures you only receive alerts that are important to you and minimizes distractions. To customize notifications, go to the settings menu and select "Notifications." Here, you can manage notification settings for each app individually. You can choose to allow or disallow notifications, set them to appear as banners, alerts, or badges, and decide whether they should appear on the lock screen or in the notification center. Additionally, you can configure notification sounds and set up notification grouping to keep your alerts organized.

Changing themes and wallpapers and customizing notifications, you can tailor the Apple Vision Pro to better reflect your style and needs, creating a more enjoyable and efficient user experience.

**Using Shortcuts and Automations**

Using shortcuts and automations on the Apple Vision Pro can greatly enhance your productivity by streamlining routine tasks. Setting Up Shortcuts involves creating custom commands that perform multiple actions automatically. To set up shortcuts, open the Shortcuts app and tap the "+" button to create a new shortcut. You can choose from a wide range of actions such as sending a message, opening an app, or controlling smart home devices. Combine these actions into a single shortcut by adding each step in the desired order. Once your shortcut is set up, you can run it by tapping the shortcut icon, asking Siri, or creating a home screen widget for quick access. This allows you to perform complex tasks with a single command, saving time and effort.

Automating Routine Tasks takes shortcuts a step further by triggering them based on specific conditions or times. To set up automations, open the Shortcuts app, go to the "Automation" tab, and tap the "+" button to create a new automation. You can set triggers such as a specific time of day, arriving at or leaving a location, or connecting to a Wi-Fi network. Once you've chosen a trigger, select the actions you want to automate. For example, you can set up an automation to turn on Do Not Disturb mode and dim the screen when you connect to your home Wi-Fi in the evening. Automations run automatically based on the conditions you set, further simplifying your daily routines. By setting up shortcuts and automations, you can make your Apple Vision Pro work more efficiently for you, reducing the need for repetitive manual actions and enhancing your overall user experience.

# Chapter 9:
# Troubleshooting and
# Support

**Common Issues and Solutions**

Connectivity problems and performance issues are common concerns for users of the Apple Vision Pro.

Connectivity Problems can include difficulties connecting to Wi-Fi, Bluetooth, or other devices. To troubleshoot Wi-Fi issues, ensure that your router is functioning properly and that you are within range. Restarting your device and router can often resolve connectivity issues. Check that your Wi-Fi settings are correct by navigating to "Settings," then "Wi-Fi," and selecting your network. If problems persist, forget the network and reconnect by entering the password again. For Bluetooth issues, ensure that the device you are trying to connect to is in pairing mode and that Bluetooth is enabled on your Vision Pro. Restarting both devices and re-pairing them can help resolve connectivity problems.

Performance Issues such as slow operation, app crashes, or unresponsiveness can be addressed with a few steps. First, ensure your device is running the latest software version by going to "Settings," then "General," and selecting "Software Update." Closing unused apps can free up system resources and improve performance. To close apps, swipe up from the bottom of the screen and pause in the middle, then swipe up on the app previews. Restarting your device can also resolve minor performance issues. If the problem persists, check your storage usage under "Settings," then "General," and "iPhone Storage" (or equivalent). Deleting unused apps and files can free up space and improve performance. For persistent issues, consider resetting your settings by going to "Settings," then "General," and selecting "Reset," then "Reset All Settings." By following these troubleshooting steps, you can address common connectivity and performance issues, ensuring your Apple Vision Pro operates smoothly and efficiently.

**Accessing Support Resources**

Accessing support resources for the Apple Vision Pro is essential when you encounter issues that you cannot resolve on your own. Using the Help App provides immediate access to a wealth of information and troubleshooting tips. Open the Help app on your Apple Vision Pro to search for topics related to your issue. The app includes guides, FAQs, and detailed instructions on various features and common problems. You can browse by category or use the search function to find specific information. This self-help resource is designed to provide quick and easy solutions without the need for external assistance.

Contacting Apple Support is necessary for more complex issues or when the Help app does not resolve your problem. To contact Apple Support, go to the settings menu and select "Support." You will be directed to options such as chat support, scheduling a call, or making an appointment at the nearest Apple Store or authorized service provider. Apple Support can assist with hardware and software issues, provide guidance on warranty and repair options, and offer personalized troubleshooting steps. Having your device's serial number and a detailed description of your issue ready will help expedite the support process.

Using the Help app and contacting Apple Support when needed, you can access comprehensive support resources to address and resolve any issues with your Apple Vision Pro efficiently.

**Maintenance and Updates**

Keeping your Apple Vision Pro up to date and performing regular maintenance are crucial for optimal performance and longevity. Keeping Your Device Up to Date involves regularly checking for and installing software updates. To do this, go to "Settings," then "General," and select "Software Update." If an update is available, follow the on-screen instructions to download and install it. Software updates often include new features, security patches, and performance improvements, ensuring your device runs smoothly and securely.

Performing Regular Maintenance helps maintain the device's performance and extends its lifespan. Regularly restart your Apple Vision Pro to clear temporary files and refresh the system. Check your storage usage by going to "Settings," then "General," and selecting "iPhone Storage" (or equivalent). Delete unused apps, old files, and cache to free up space. Keep your screen and sensors clean by using a microfiber cloth and avoid using harsh chemicals. Additionally, ensure that all apps are updated by checking the App Store regularly for updates. Monitoring battery health in the "Battery" section of the settings can also help you manage usage and charging habits to prolong battery life. Kkeeping your device up to date and performing regular maintenance, you can ensure that your Apple Vision Pro operates efficiently and remains in good condition for years to come.

# Chapter 10: Tips and Tricks

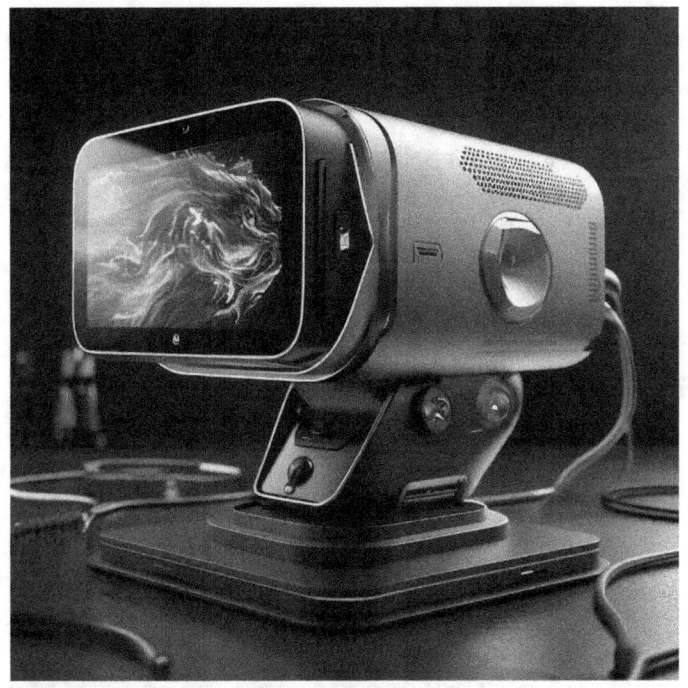

**Maximizing Battery Life**

Maximizing battery life on your Apple Vision Pro involves several practical steps. First, adjust your screen brightness to a lower level, which can significantly reduce battery consumption. You can do this by swiping down from the top-right corner to access the Control Center and adjusting the brightness slider. Enabling auto-brightness in the settings under "Display & Brightness" also helps, as it adjusts the screen brightness based on ambient light conditions.

Next, manage your app usage by closing apps running in the background that you are not actively using. Double-tap the home button or swipe up from the bottom of the screen and pause in the middle to see all open apps, then swipe up on the apps you want to close. Additionally, disable unnecessary push notifications and background app refresh. Go to "Settings," then

"Notifications," and turn off notifications for apps that don't require immediate attention. For background app refresh, navigate to "Settings," "General," and "Background App Refresh," and select apps that should not refresh content when not in use. Using Low Power Mode can also help extend battery life. This mode reduces power consumption by disabling or limiting certain features like mail fetch, background app refresh, and some visual effects. You can enable Low Power Mode in the Control Center or by going to "Settings," then "Battery," and toggling it on.

Lastly, optimize your settings by turning off Wi-Fi, Bluetooth, and GPS when not in use. Access these options from the Control Center or through their respective settings menus. Keeping your device's software updated also ensures that you have the latest improvements and bug fixes that can enhance battery performance. By following these tips, you can maximize the battery life of your Apple Vision Pro, ensuring it lasts throughout the day.

**Enhancing Performance**

Enhancing the performance of your Apple Vision Pro involves several key practices to ensure the device operates smoothly and efficiently. First, regularly restart your device to clear temporary files and refresh the system, which can help improve speed and responsiveness. To restart, press and hold the power button until the "slide to power off" slider appears, then slide to turn off, and press the power button again to turn it back on. Keeping your software up to date is crucial for maintaining performance. Check for updates by going to "Settings," then "General," and selecting "Software Update." Install any available updates to benefit from the latest enhancements and security patches.

Managing storage effectively also plays a significant role in device performance. Go to "Settings," then "General," and select "iPhone Storage" (or equivalent) to see a breakdown of your storage usage. Delete unused apps, old files, and large attachments that you no longer need. Consider using cloud services like iCloud to store photos and videos, freeing up space on your device. Limiting background activities can further enhance performance. Disable Background App Refresh for apps that do not need to update content in the background. Navigate to "Settings," then "General," and "Background App Refresh" to customize which apps can refresh in the background. Additionally, reduce the number of widgets and dynamic wallpapers, as these can consume resources and slow down your device.

Finally, regularly clear your browser cache and cookies by going to "Settings," selecting your browser, and choosing the option to clear history and website data. This can improve browsing speed and overall device performance. By following these steps, you can enhance the performance of your Apple Vision Pro, ensuring it runs efficiently and provides a smooth user experience.

**Hidden Features and Hacks**

Exploring hidden features and hacks on the Apple Vision Pro can unlock additional functionality and enhance your user experience. One useful feature is the ability to customize Control Center, giving you quick access to the tools you use most. Go to "Settings," select "Control Center," and tap "Customize Controls." From here, you can add, remove, and rearrange controls to suit your preferences. This makes it easier to access features like screen recording, low power mode, and more.

Another handy hack is using the "Back Tap" feature for quick shortcuts. Go to "Settings," then "Accessibility," select "Touch," and choose "Back Tap." You can set a double or triple tap on the back of your device to perform actions like taking a screenshot, opening Control Center, or launching specific apps. This feature is particularly useful for quickly accessing frequently used functions.

For a more efficient typing experience, you can enable the one-handed keyboard. This is especially useful on larger devices. To activate it, press and hold the globe or emoji icon on the keyboard and select either the left or right-handed keyboard icon. This shifts the keyboard closer to the thumb of the chosen hand, making it easier to type with one hand.

The "Measure" app, often overlooked, turns your device into a digital measuring tape. Open the app and use your device's camera to measure objects and distances accurately. This is especially useful for quick measurements without needing a physical tape measure. Additionally, you can use "Siri Shortcuts" to automate common tasks. Open the Shortcuts app and create custom shortcuts that combine multiple actions. For example, you can create a shortcut that sends a message, sets a reminder, and opens a navigation app with a single voice command. By exploring these hidden features and hacks, you can make the most of your Apple Vision Pro, enhancing both functionality and convenience in your daily use.

# Conclusion

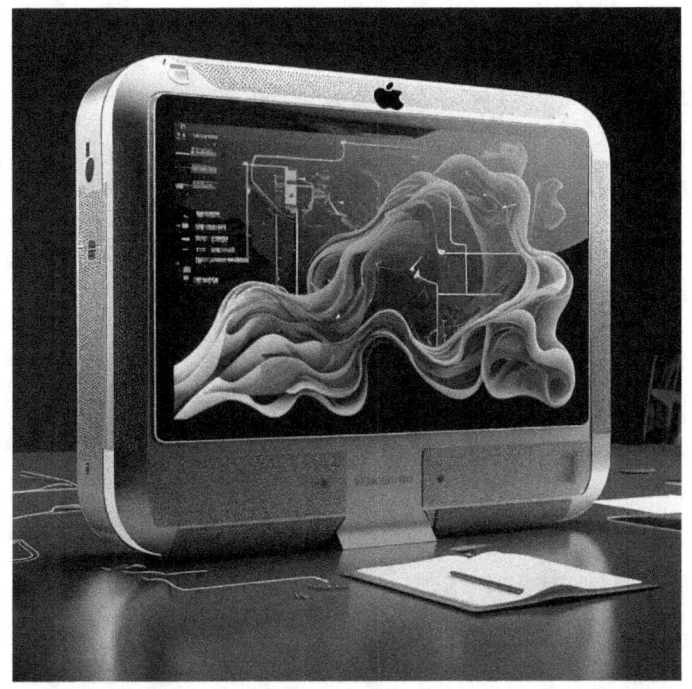

"Mastering Apple Vision Pro - The Ultimate User's Guide: Step-by-Step Instructions to Get Started" has provided a detailed roadmap to help you fully harness the capabilities of your Apple Vision Pro. From the initial setup and configuration to exploring advanced features and troubleshooting common issues, this guide aims to ensure that you can maximize your device's potential. By familiarizing yourself with the core functionalities, such as augmented reality experiences, media consumption, and productivity tools, you can enhance both your personal and professional life.

The comprehensive overview of security and privacy settings empowers you to protect your data, while the tips on performance optimization and battery management ensure your device remains efficient and reliable. Customizing your user experience through settings, shortcuts, and automations allows you to tailor the Apple Vision Pro to your specific needs, making daily tasks more streamlined and enjoyable. The inclusion of hidden features and hacks offers additional ways to improve your interaction with the device, unlocking new levels of convenience and functionality.

In summary, this guide serves as a thorough resource for both novice and experienced users, offering clear and practical advice to navigate and utilize the Apple Vision Pro. By leveraging the information and tips provided, you can confidently explore the full range of possibilities this innovative technology offers, ensuring you get the most out of your investment. Whether for work, play, or personal growth, mastering your Apple Vision Pro opens up a world of opportunities, enhancing your digital experience in profound ways.